PRO WRESTLING LEGENDS

Steve Austin
The Story of the Wrestler They Call "Stone Cold"

Bill Goldberg

Bret Hart
The Story of the Wrestler They Call "The Hitman"

The Story of the Wrestler
They Call "Hollywood" Hulk Hogan

Randy Savage
The Story of the Wrestler They Call "Macho Man"

The Story of the Wrestler They Call "Sting"

The Story of the Wrestler They Call "The Undertaker"

Jesse Ventura
The Story of the Wrestler They Call "The Body"

CHELSEA HOUSE PUBLISHERS

The Story of the Wrestler They Call "Hollywood" Hulk Hogan

Matt Hunter

Chelsea House Publishers
Philadelphia

Produced by Choptank Syndicate, Inc.

Editor and Picture Researcher: Mary Hull
Design and Production: Lisa Hochstein

CHELSEA HOUSE PUBLISHERS

Editor in Chief: Stephen Reginald
Managing Editor: James D. Gallagher
Production Manager: Pamela Loos
Art Director: Sara Davis
Director of Photography: Judy L. Hasday
Senior Production Editor: LeeAnne Gelletly
Cover Illustrator: Keith Trego

Cover Photos: WCW
              Sports Action

The Chelsea House World Wide Web site
address is http://www.chelseahouse.com

First Printing

1 3 5 7 9 8 6 4 2

Library of Congress Cataloging-in-Publication Data

Hunter, Matt.
    The story of the wrestler they call "Hollywood" Hulk Hogan / Matt Hunter.
        p. cm.—(Pro wrestling legends)
    Includes bibliographical references (p.) and index.
    Summary: A biography of the professional superstar wrestler known as
"Hollywood" Hulk Hogan.
    ISBN 0-7910-5406-3 (hard.) — ISBN 0-7910-5552-3 (pbk.)
    1.Hogan, Hulk, 1955–   Juvenile literature. 2. Wrestlers—United States—
Biography—Juvenile literature. [1. Hogan, Hulk, 1955–   . 2. Wrestlers.]
I. Title. II. Series.
GV1196.H64H86 1999
796.812'092—dc21
    [B]   99-16449
                                                                 CIP

Contents

1 HULKAMANIA BORN!

Anybody who was in New York's Madison Square Garden on the evening of January 23, 1984, can consider themselves remarkably fortunate. Because that was one of the landmark dates in pro wrestling history, the night pro wrestling entered a new era, the night a new World Wrestling Federation (WWF) World heavyweight champion was crowned—and the night Hulkamania was born.

At the time, the Iron Sheik was WWF World heavyweight champion, having brought the four-year reign of Bob Backlund to an end just five weeks earlier in the same Madison Square Garden ring.

Managed by Fred Blassie, the Sheik was one of the most hated men in professional wrestling. His title-winning match against the immensely popular Backlund resulted in controversy (Backlund's manager, Arnold Skaaland, had thrown in the towel on behalf of his man) and injury (Backlund's back was hurt as the result of being caught in the Sheik's "camel clutch" submission hold, which pins the victim prone on the mat with his legs bent painfully behind his back).

Ordinarily, Backlund would have been the recipient of a return title match the following month in Madison Square Garden, but his back injury was too severe. It's not unusual

Hulkamania, the pro wrestling revival that swept the nation, was born the night Hulk Hogan defeated the Iron Sheik for the WWF World heavyweight title on January 23, 1984.

for wrestlers to compete when they are injured, and Backlund did, in fact, campaign for the title match. Nevertheless, the WWF commissioners who had the power to sign main events denied the former champion's requests.

They had another challenger in mind.

Hulk Hogan had wrestled in the WWF before. As a rulebreaker in 1980 and 1981, Hogan had challenged then-WWF World champion Backlund on several occasions. Though he had come short of winning the title, Hogan had impressed fans worldwide with a power-based offense that made the most of his 6' 8" self. He had also impressed the world by bodyslamming 525-pound Andre the Giant during a televised bout, thereby accomplishing what many felt was an impossible goal.

After leaving the WWF in 1981, Hogan wrestled in the American Wrestling Association (AWA) and in Japan. Toward the end of 1983, Hogan was spending most of his time chasing the AWA World title. Though the AWA is no longer in existence, the AWA World title was viewed, in the mid-1980s, as one of the most coveted championships in the entire world.

When Hogan grew weary of wrestling in the AWA, he turned his gaze eastward toward the WWF. Backlund's loss to the Sheik had not gone unnoticed by Hogan, and on December 27, 1983—just one day after Backlund's title fell to the Sheik—Hogan returned to the WWF.

Before long, the news spread throughout the wrestling world: Hogan was declared the number one contender for the WWF World heavyweight title.

WWF wrestlers cried foul. WWF fans cried foul. Most of all, Blassie and Shiek cried foul.

Bob Backlund was supposed to get the title shot at the Iron Sheik at Madison Square Garden on January 23, 1984, but a back injury sidelined him and WWF commissioners gave Hulk Hogan the chance instead.

The reason for the uproar was that Hogan had not even wrestled a match in the WWF when he was named top contender. On one side of the argument, it was said that Hogan deserved the top placement on the basis of his past performance in the WWF and his recent matches in the AWA. On the other side of the argument, it was said that Hogan needed to work his way up the ladder of contention—that he needed to gain at least a few victories over important WWF competitors before being considered for a title match.

The argument, however, was beside the point. The WWF officials had made their decision, and

Hogan would wrestle the Sheik for the title on January 23, 1984.

Madison Square Garden was sold out for the match as more than 20,000 fans packed the legendary building to see Hogan and the Sheik wage war. Another 4,000 fans purchased tickets to watch the bout via closed circuit television at the Felt Forum, a small arena adjacent to the Garden. The atmosphere in midtown Manhattan was nothing short of electric, and the undercard (secondary matches) to the main event seemed almost incidental.

Speculation was running rampant prior to the match. After all, the Sheik, the defending champion, was being managed by Fred Blassie, who had managed Hogan during his WWF tenure as a rulebreaker. The relationship between manager and wrestler is a close one, with the manager knowing most, if not all, of the wrestler's strengths, weaknesses, and secrets. Questions about Blassie and Sheik prompted plenty of prematch debate:

How much did Blassie really know about Hogan?

How much of his knowledge had he passed along to the Sheik?

If Hogan had failed so often in his title quest against Bockwinkel, how did he think he could be successful against Sheik?

How could Hogan, possessing an admittedly limited wrestling repertoire, actually prevail against Sheik, who had represented Iran in the Olympic Games?

With all of the controversy surrounding his number one contender position, could Hogan maintain the mental focus necessary to wrestle well?

As it turned out, it took only five minutes and 40 seconds to answer all those questions.

Those who witnessed it live described it as nothing short of a massacre.

The Sheik incited the crowd by waving the Iranian flag and shouting, "Iran! Number one! Iran! Number one!" Blassie grinned. The crowd jeered and booed. Hatred for the Sheik was easy to come by: the memories of the 14-month Iranian-hostage crisis, which had ended three years earlier, were still fresh in everyone's mind. The Sheik might as well have been the Ayatollah Khomeini himself.

Then came the thunderous sounds of "Eye of the Tiger," a Survivor song made popular in the *Rocky* movies and chosen by Hogan as his theme. In 1984 theme music for a professional wrestler was still relatively rare, and the familiar chords took Blassie and the Sheik by surprise.

(Nearly a decade later, Hogan said in an interview in the *Nashville Network* that he'd snuck up to the sound booth at Madison Square Garden and, against the wishes of WWF owner Vince McMahon Jr., paid several hundred dollars to the technician to play the music.)

As the crowd cheered their welcome, Hogan stormed to the ring. A spectacularly charismatic sight, Hogan was American patriotism person-ified, propelled by muscular legs boasting 31-inch thighs. Hogan's 60-inch chest glistened with sweat and his 24-inch biceps were primed for action.

Neither the crowd nor the Sheik had much of a chance to catch a breath!

Hogan was a whirlwind of fury, tossing the Sheik around the ring the way a cat would play with a toy, much to the delight of the fans. On a grand scale, it was as if all the frustrations of the United States toward Iran were wrapped up in this one match. On a more personal scale, it was Hogan's golden opportunity to seize the spotlight for himself.

The spotlight was as blinding as the speed with which Hogan dispatched the Sheik. After five minutes of spectacularly one-sided action, Hogan catapulted the Sheik into the ropes. The Sheik rebounded, only to be met square in the face by Hogan's boot.

The Sheik fell to the mat, stunned. He didn't see Hogan hurl himself against the far ropes. He didn't see Hogan launch his 300-pound physique into the air. But he did feel the mighty legdrop that thundered into his chest and,

Nobody liked the Iron Sheik, whose anti-American ways aroused the wrath of wrestling fans. When Hulk Hogan defeated the Sheik in front of 20,000 fans at New York's Madison Square Garden, Hogan became an American hero.

at the 5:40 mark, ended his WWF World title reign.

Even the referee, in all likelihood, didn't hear his hand slap the mat a third time. The sound of the cheering in Madison Square Garden was deafening. The fans—more than 20,000 strong—gave Hogan a standing ovation!

Once again, the powerful chords of "Eye of the Tiger" filled the arena, mixing with the cheers and creating an energy that is rarely seen in any sport. It all focused on the man in the ring, the man who was holding the belt high in the air, the man who had finally won a World heavyweight title.

Hulk Hogan had given it his all, and the fans were giving him their love, their honor, and their respect. The cheering went on for what seemed like an eternity as the wrestling world crowned not just a new champion, but a new hero.

Hulkamania was born that night in New York City, and it became an amazing force that quickly spread across the nation and around the world.

But it took nearly 30 years for Hulk Hogan to achieve pro wrestling glory the likes of which few wrestlers have ever known. That glory was sweet for Hulk Hogan, whose early years had been marked by more than his fair share of struggle and turmoil.

THE RING BECKONS

The man who would change the face of professional wrestling in the 1980s and 1990s, make the cover of *Sports Illustrated* magazine in 1985, and become a worldwide celebrity, was born Terry Bollea on August 11, 1953, in Augusta, Georgia. When Terry was young, his family moved to Tampa, Florida, which is the city he has long called home.

Terry's father, Pete, was a construction foreman, while his mother, Ruth, was a homemaker. For Ruth, it was her second marriage; Terry has a half brother, Kenneth Wheeler, from Ruth's first marriage. He also had a full brother, Allan, now deceased.

In addition to keeping the Bollea household running, Ruth was also a dance teacher, and told *People* magazine in 1991 that "Terry gets a lot of his showmanship from me."

By the age of 12, Terry weighed 195 pounds. He didn't play sports in school, and his size made him awkward at a time in life when everything seems awkward. Indeed, big kids don't go unnoticed in the difficult proving ground of grade school. By the age of 14, Terry was fighting with fellow students so often that he wound up at the Florida Sheriff's Boys Ranch, a reform school designed to straighten out kids who were headed down the wrong path in life. Terry took advantage of his

---

In 1978, 25-year-old Terry Bollea made his pro wrestling debut in Florida and Tennessee as "Terry Boulder." One year later, Vince McMahon Sr. recruited him for the WWF, renaming him "the Incredible Hulk Hogan."

second chance and straightened himself out, becoming a born-again Baptist in the process.

He also kept growing.

"In ninth grade I weighed 240 pounds," Hogan told the *Nashville Network* in January 1993. "When I graduated from high school I was over 300 pounds and I was really fat. Then I started training because I wanted a girlfriend really bad."

Terry attended the same Tampa high school that would turn out a veritable battle royal of professional wrestlers, including Dick Slater, Steve Keirn, Mike Graham, and Brutus Beefcake; to this day, Hogan and Beefcake remain very close friends. But wrestling wasn't in Terry's plans when he graduated from high school. He wanted to be a musician.

Terry played bass guitar, and his band played the Tampa bar and nightclub circuit. When he wasn't playing music, he worked as a bouncer. When he wasn't working, he was working out. Along the way, he attended business classes at Hillsborough Community College and the University of South Florida. Perhaps he was preparing for a future in the music business, but fate had a different plan for Terry Bollea.

"I was still bouncing around the same old clubs for eight or nine years," he told the *Nashville Network*. "But when I heard about how much darn money the wrestlers made, and I watched these guys every night come into the bar I was playing at, and I said, 'How can these guys wrestle every day and stay out all night every night?' I made friends with some of the wrestlers. At first I was intimidated [but] once I got around them—I was always big and into

Ed Leslie, aka Brutus "the Barber" Beefcake, went to high school with Terry Bollea in Tampa, Florida. The two friends later decided to try pro wrestling, and they competed in tag team matches as the brothers "Terry and Ed Boulder."

working out—and one thing led to another and here I am."

The one thing that led to another was Hogan meeting legendary Florida-area wrestlers Jack and Jerry Brisco. Both were highly accomplished pro wrestlers. Jack had captured the National Wrestling Alliance (NWA) World title twice, in 1973 and 1974; together, the brothers would go on to win three NWA World tag team championships in the early 1980s.

The Briscos, both highly regarded experts in the scientific skills of the mat sport, saw potential in the massive Terry Bollea. He had the size (approximately 6' 8" and nearly 300 pounds by this time), he had the look (all muscles and long blond hair), and he had a natural charisma that came from his own personality and from the comfort of being on stage playing bass with his various rock bands. The Briscos asked Terry if he'd ever considered a career in the pro wrestling ring. He replied that he'd wanted to become a pro wrestler all his life.

Right answer.

Terry began training with Jack and Jerry, and also with legendary Japanese wrestler Hiro Matsuda. He learned the scientific skills of the sport, and he learned how to use his massive size to his advantage. After about six months, he was ready to step into the ring.

In 1978, Terry made his pro debut under the name "Terry Boulder." The details of those early matches are lost in the haze of wrestling history, but one detail remains clear: Terry's natural charisma was undeniable. "By the time he got into the ring, he was getting a standing ovation," Jerry Brisco recalls. "Nobody had a clue who this was, but they were cheering him like he was already a superstar."

The cheers were a bit premature, as Hogan would soon become one of the most hated men in the sport.

Terry spent about a year paying his dues in Florida and Tennessee, wrestling as Terry "The Hulk" Boulder and Sterling Golden. When he wasn't competing in singles bouts, he wrestled in tag team matches with his "brother" Eddie Boulder, who was actually his longtime friend,

Ed Leslie, who would later go on to become Brutus Beefcake. For all the work, Terry was earning about $125 for wrestling seven nights a week.

The work paid off, and Terry's big break came.

In 1979, Terry was recruited by Vince McMahon Sr., father of current WWF owner Vince McMahon Jr. The elder McMahon promoted WWF events primarily in the Northeast, and dubbed Terry "the Incredible Hulk Hogan," playing off the title of the then-popular *Incredible Hulk* television series starring bodybuilder Lou Ferrigno.

Hogan's size astounded WWF fans, whose eyeballs were used to seeing WWF World champion Bob Backlund—6' 1" and 234 pounds—as the federation's standard-bearer. The astonishment turned to hatred when the fans realized Hogan was managed by the despised rule-breaking manager Fred Blassie.

Main-event matches were still to come, but Hogan was fast building his reputation. His egotistical interviews about his strength and good looks, underscored by Blassie's growling diatribes, made him the most hated man in the WWF. The fact that he was winning all of his matches helped fuel the ire of fans as well. A successful feud with popular muscleman "Mr. USA" Tony Atlas landed Hogan on the covers of national wrestling publications and added to his growing legend.

The winning didn't continue for long, but the reputation was about to grow considerably.

In 1980, the WWF decided to match its two biggest men: Hulk Hogan and Andre the Giant. A legend for years, Andre was an undeniable superstar. His massive size—nearly seven feet in height and 500 pounds!—made him the immovable object in a wrestling world of irresistible forces.

But Andre wasn't immovable.

When Hogan bodyslammed Andre during a televised bout, the wrestling fans of the nation were shocked and stunned . . . and they wanted more. A series of Andre-Hogan bouts followed, culminating in an August 8, 1980, bout in New York's Shea Stadium.

The Shea Stadium card remains legendary. It broke all box-office records of the day, drawing 35,771 fans to the ballpark the New York Mets baseball team calls home. In the main

At seven feet tall and 500 pounds, Andre the Giant made an imposing foe for Hulk Hogan, and WWF promoters were anxious to schedule a bout between the two wrestlers. Hogan lost to Andre during an August 8, 1980, match that drew a record crowd to New York's Shea Stadium.

event Bruno Sammartino defeated former student Larry Zbyszko in a cage match. In the other major bout on the card Hulk Hogan battled Andre the Giant.

Hogan lost by pinfall in front of the largest crowd ever to see wrestling up to that time.

Ouch.

Retreating to Japan, Hogan continued his rulebreaking ways. He won matches, but longed to return to the States to prove himself and make up for the loss to Andre. After several months he did return to the WWF, again under the management of Blassie, and again as a hated rulebreaker.

Blassie lobbied hard for World title matches for his charge, but champion Bob Backlund and his manager, Arnold Skaaland, weren't granting them so readily. Blassie charged that Backlund was ducking Hogan out of fear; Backlund countered that there were many challengers to his title, and the WWF promoters and officials, not the WWF champion, decided who his opponents would be.

Finally, the WWF relented and Hulk Hogan got his title shot against Backlund . . . in New Haven, Connecticut. Hogan was outraged! He felt the match should have been held in Madison Square Garden, the crown jewel of the arenas in which the WWF promoted. By signing the match for New Haven, Hogan felt, the WWF had dealt him a despicable insult.

Backlund retained his title in the bout, but Hogan was too angry to worry about lobbying for rematches. He left the WWF behind, along with his rulebreaking tendencies and the jeers of the fans.

His destiny was right around the corner.

3 READY FOR PRIME TIME

In 1981, professional wrestling in the United States was far more fragmented than it is today. Ted Turner's World Championship Wrestling (WCW) didn't exist. The most influential organization at the time was the NWA, a group of regional promotions dominated by Jim Crockett Promotions, which was based in the Carolinas. The WWF was strong, though it was mainly a regional promotion based in the Northeast. In the number-three spot was the AWA, based out of Minneapolis.

The AWA boasted stars like Verne Gagne, the Crusher, Nick Bockwinkel, and Mad Dog Vachon. Their tag team champions were duos like Crusher and Dick the Bruiser, Blackjack Lanza and Bobby Duncum, and Greg Gagne and Jim Brunzell.

The fans in the AWA had never seen a star like Hulk Hogan.

Hogan arrived in the AWA in the autumn of 1981. Managed by the cigar-chomping Johnny Valiant, Hogan initially mimicked his rulebreaking ways from the WWF, but the fans would have none of it. The cheers rained down as Hogan competed, and before long he was a full-fledged fan favorite.

He became the AWA's biggest box-office draw of all time. The Hulk Hogan juggernaut was beginning to roll.

As reigning WWF World champion and the biggest star that wrestling had ever known, Hulk Hogan represented all-American values. Acting as a role model for the nation's children, he told them to say their prayers, take their vitamins, and always play fair.

In the AWA, Hogan used his powerful offensive skills and unparalleled fan support to propel himself to victory in feuds with "Crusher" Jerry Blackwell and Jesse "The Body" Ventura. He wrestled Bockwinkel for the AWA World title several times, but never captured the belt, and even ventured out of the AWA on several occasions to battle NWA World champion Harley Race. To Hogan, however, the AWA and NWA belts didn't necessarily matter. If he wasn't successful as a champion in the States, well, he could always go back to Japan and wrestle. So he did.

Professional wrestling in Japan has always been enormously popular, on par with pro football or baseball in the United States. In the early 1980s, while wrestling in the AWA, Hogan made repeated trips to Japan, and it was there that he tasted his first championship gold by defeating the legendary Antonio Inoki on June 2, 1983, for the IWGP (International Wrestling Grand Prix) heavyweight title. He held the championship for more than a year before losing it back to Inoki on June 14, 1984.

In the meantime, opportunity knocked outside the wrestling ring. Sylvester Stallone was looking for a powerful and photogenic professional wrestler to appear in *Rocky III*. Hogan landed the part of Thunderlips—the Ultimate Male, and *Rocky III* went on to become a major hit. Hogan's popularity was soaring, and he even landed a guest spot on *The Tonight Show* with Johnny Carson.

Back in the AWA, Hogan's career was thriving, too. He collected $10,000 and enhanced his reputation by bodyslamming 474-pound Crusher Blackwell. He defeated Bockwinkel in a no-disqualification match—and held the AWA

In the 1980s Hulk Hogan promoted the connection between Hollywood, rock music, and professional wrestling by appearing with celebrities like singer Cyndi Lauper.

title for 20 minutes before AWA officials claimed that the disqualification rule could not be waived for a title match. Hogan's interest in AWA activities, though, was waning as his repuation continued to grow.

It became clear that the AWA didn't quite know how to handle their superstar, and Hogan was outgrowing the AWA very quickly. For a brief time, riding the popularity of *Rocky III*, Hogan considered giving up wrestling for Hollywood. But events in the sport were conspiring to make Hogan the biggest star wrestling had ever known.

In 1983, Vince McMahon Jr. was beginning to take the reins of control at the WWF over from his father. McMahon was not about to sit still and promote wrestling the way it had been promoted for the past 50 years. He knew he wanted to take the sport in a new direction. That meant new faces, new promotional methods, and a new way of thinking. No longer would pro wrestling be a regional business. McMahon was going to take the sport, infuse it with modern marketing ideas, and place it on a national—and international—stage.

Hulk Hogan was going to be his leader in doing so.

In November 1983, while wrestling in Japan, Hogan was signed to a WWF contract by Vince McMahon Sr. The signing, which went virtually unreported in the wrestling press, was the first step in a two-month series of events that would rock the wrestling world and put Vince McMahon Jr. in a superb position to start realizing his dreams of global marketing dominance for the WWF.

On December 26, 1983, Bob Backlund's four-year WWF World title reign was ended by the Iron Sheik.

On December 27, 1983, Hulk Hogan made his reappearance in the WWF, appearing at a television taping.

In early January 1984, WWF officials denied a title rematch to Backlund, who had been injured in his loss to the Sheik.

Days later, WWF officials granted the title match with Sheik to Hogan. It would take place on January 23, 1984, in Madison Square Garden.

WWF wrestlers were outraged. Hogan had wrestled only one match in the WWF since his December return, and that was a tag team bout. What did he do to deserve the coveted title match?

It didn't matter. The match was set, and the federation that had insulted him years before by relegating his title match to New Haven, Connecticut, welcomed him back to Madison Square Garden with open arms.

So did the fans, who cheered his astonishing victory over the Iron Sheik in a way that is reserved for only the most incredible moments in all of sports. New York hosted a Garden party on January 23, and Hogan was the guest of honor.

The date marked the official beginning of Hulkamania and ushered in a new era for professional wrestling. Hogan's initial title defenses were made against Samoans Afa and Sika, "Mr. Wonderful" Paul Orndorff, and "Dr. D" David Shultz. But title defenses seemed secondary to WWF fans, who simply wanted to bask in the glow of Hulkamania, a seemingly irresistible force that stood for all-American values: saying one's prayers, taking one's vitamins, and observing sportsmanship and fair play at every turn.

It was a platform upon which McMahon was able to build, and build he did. With Hogan at the forefront, the WWF expanded nationwide. Regional promoters who had spent years observing unwritten rules that said "I won't promote in your city, and you won't promote in mine" suddenly saw that the unwritten rules didn't matter anymore. As Hogan steamrolled over opponents in the ring, racking up victory after victory with a big foot to the face and a legdrop, McMahon steamrolled over promoters out of the ring, racking up sellout after arena

The entertainment aspect of pro wrestling was enhanced by events like the first Wrestlemania, which featured Liberace as timekeeper and Muhammed Ali as guest referee for a match pitting Hogan and Mr. T against "Rowdy" Roddy Piper and Paul "Mr. Wonderful" Orndorff on March 31, 1985.

sellout by signing the biggest stars of regional promotions to the WWF, often luring them with promises of a title shot against Hogan.

As 1984 drew to a close, the mainstream media began to notice Hogan and the WWF in a big way. True, they didn't care much when Hogan successfully defended his title against Big John Studd in October. But when former rock band bassist Hogan began defending the rock 'n' roll lifestyle, which was being criticized by "Rowdy" Roddy Piper, reporters started taking notice.

So did MTV, which televised a February 18, 1985, Madison Square Garden bout between Hogan and Piper. The contest was known as "The War to Settle the Score," and the "Hulkster" won by disqualification when actor Mr. T (whose *A-Team* television series was immensely popular) and rock star Cyndi Lauper (whose album *She's So Unusual* spawned four Top-Five singles in 1984) interfered.

The Rock 'n' Wrestling connection that would define pro wrestling in the mid-1980s was born. Next stop: WrestleMania.

The first WrestleMania card was held March 31, 1985, in Madison Square Garden. Though not available on pay-per-view television at the time, it was made available to 135 closed-circuit television locations and drew an estimated viewership of 400,000 fans.

The main event of the first WrestleMania, as was the case with so many subsequent WrestleManias, revolved around Hogan. The Hulkster teamed with Mr. T to battle Piper and Paul Orndorff. Hogan and Mr. T claimed victory when Hogan pinned Orndorff, but the real story of WrestleMania was the level of mainstream celebrity involvement. Cyndi Lauper managed Wendi Richter to a WWF World women's championship victory over Lelani Kai. Former New York Yankees manager Billy Martin was on hand as a guest ring announcer. Entertainment legend Liberace was guest timekeeper for the main event. Legendary boxer Muhammad Ali was special outside-the-ring referee for the main event.

In the audience, too, celebrities were seen everywhere. Suddenly, pro wrestling was on everybody's "in" list. Just as movers and shakers like to be seen at the biggest fights in boxing, those same movers and shakers were burning up the phones trying to secure the best possible tickets for WrestleMania.

Hogan was seen everywhere, too. Talk shows clamored for him to be a guest, and he appeared with Cyndi Lauper at the 1985 Grammy Awards program.

It might have happened without Hulk Hogan. If there had been no Hulkster, it can be argued, there might have been someone else to take wrestling to a new level of popularity. But Hogan was in the right place at the right time, and it's impossible to imagine any other wrestler thriving to such a remarkable degree under the incredible glare of the national spotlight the way Hogan did.

WrestleMania seemed big enough, but there would quickly be more. On May 11, 1985, pro wrestling returned to network television for the first time in 30 years as WWF's *Saturday Night's Main Event* premiered on NBC. The main event was reminiscent of WrestleMania as Hogan battled and defeated "Cowboy" Bob Orton with Piper, Mr. T, and Orndorff at ringside.

With every passing day, Hogan's star grew brighter. He was becoming a genuine phenomenon.

"I'm not a politician or a great thinker," Hogan said. "I'm a wrestler. If I can rid the sport of those who don't believe in giving people a fair chance, I can show the world the American dream isn't dead."

Hogan spouted all-American values in his interviews, and those values were reflected in his ring entrance theme song "Eye of the Tiger" by Survivor:

> I am a real American
> Fight for the rights of every man
> I am a real American

Fight for what's right
Fight for your life.

The words were inspirational to Hulkamaniacs, but Hogan didn't need to fight for his
life. He was the biggest star the sport had ever
known. Bigger than Gorgeous George, Buddy
Rogers, or Bruno Sammartino in their respec-
tive heydays. Bigger than most mainstream
sports stars and mainstream entertainment
celebrities in the mid-1980s. He was like
Muhammad Ali, Mickey Mantle, and Joe Namath
all rolled into one.

It was only logical that Hollywood would
come calling.

4

HOLLYWOOD OR
THE RING?

The Rock 'n' Wrestling connection didn't make pro wrestling popular. After all, long before Cyndi Lauper stepped onto a wrestling ring apron, Madison Square Garden was enjoying monthly sellouts for the mat sport year after year.

What the Rock 'n' Wrestling connection did, though, was change the audience that attended wrestling and increase the amount of mainstream media attention directed toward the mat sport.

A large part of that change was due to Hogan.

"Can I take credit for this?" Hogan said in a 1993 interview when asked to look back on the Rock 'n' Wrestling connection. "I think what we were looking for when I went back to work for Vince McMahon and the WWF was to entertain the people and not insult their intelligence. Turn it from arguing if it's real or not to telling people it's 'sports entertainment'—it's acting, it's charisma, it's great athletes, it's all of the above. We were looking to entertain the people. Slowly but surely, instead of the cigar smokers and beer drinkers at ringside, I'd look out and all of a sudden I saw families out there, so it changed the face of what wrestling was."

McMahon had a great marketing idea, to be sure, but Hogan was the perfect athlete to execute that idea. He took

---

In the 1993 film Mr. Nanny, *Hulk Hogan played Sean Armstrong, a pro wrestler-turned-bodyguard who has been hired to protect two wealthy children.*

the idea and ran with it . . . and ran . . . and ran . . . and the fans loved it.

Records were shattered with stunning regularity.

On August 28, 1986, in Toronto, Ontario, Hulk Hogan successfully defended his WWF World title against "Mr. Wonderful" Paul Orndorff. It wasn't a pay-per-view event, but it probably should have been: the card drew 74,080 fans to Exhibition Stadium.

WrestleMania III on March 29, 1987, drew 93,173 fans to the Pontiac Silverdome in Pontiac, Michigan. The main event saw Hulk Hogan successfully defend his WWF World title against Andre the Giant. The live gate was $1.6 million.

Three years later, WrestleMania VI drew 67,678 fans to the SkyDome in Toronto, Ontario, as Hogan lost his title to the Ultimate Warrior. The live gate was nearly $4 million (Canadian).

All three cards should remain firmly entrenched among the list of Top-10 biggest crowds in global pro wrestling history for a long, long time to come.

Of course, a personality as large as Hogan's could not be confined to pro wrestling. So a list of acting credits that began with *Rocky III* in 1982 soon started growing lengthier, first on the television screen and later on the big screen.

In 1985, Hogan guest-starred on an episode of the popular soap opera, *Search for Tomorrow*. He made a pair of appearances on *The A-Team*, first in November 1985 and again in March 1986. In all three instances he played himself. A year later, Hogan appeared as Starlight Starbright in an episode of Dolly Parton's short-lived television series, *Dolly*. Whatever one thinks of the roles Hogan secured, the fact of the matter is that no mainstream television program will ask a wrestler to be a guest star unless that wrestler is viewed as enormously popular beyond the ring.

It was no small measure of Hogan's popularity, either, that on February 5, 1988, pro wrestling, in the form of WWF's *Main Event*, made a return to prime-time network television—after an absence of 33 years!

Meanwhile, Hollywood came knocking, as it does to anyone or anything that reaches the level of popularity Hogan had achieved.

Hogan's enormous popularity earned him numerous network TV appearances in the 1980s. Singer Dolly Parton asked Hogan to guest-star on an episode of her 1986 ABC television series Dolly, *and even wrote a song inspired by Hogan, called "He's Got a Headlock on My Heart."*

WWF World heavy-weight champion Hulk Hogan faces off against Andre the Giant at a New York press conference to promote their upcoming match, The Main Event, *an NBC primetime special aired on February 5, 1988.* The Main Event *marked pro wrestling's first appearance on prime time network television in more than 30 years.*

Producers clamored to sign Hogan's name to a film contract.

No Holds Barred was released in 1989, and it marked the Hulkster's big screen debut. In addition to serving as executive producer for the movie, he played a character named Rip Thomas. The role was not much of a stretch. Rip, a wrestling champion who is faithful to his fans and the television network for which he wrestles, faces a conflict when Brell, head of the World Television Network, wants Rip to wrestle for him. Rip refuses. Brell stages a program, "The Battle of the Tough Guys," the winner of which is a mysterious man named Zeus. Brell spends most of the rest of the movie using Zeus as a way to get at Rip.

Ironically, the celluloid feud spilled off the screen and into the ring. Hogan and Zeus did, in fact, wrestle several times, most notably at the August 28, 1989, Survivor Series. In the main event of that pay-per-view match, Hogan

and Brutus Beefcake defeated Zeus and Randy
Savage.

The movie, though, was somewhat less successful than Hogan and Beefcake at the
Survivor Series. The *Washington Post* wrote:
"His [Hogan's] performance is as dreadful as
one might expect from a man with such limited
skills outside the ring, made worse by a story
that is at once more obvious and less inspired
than your average WrestleMania script."

It didn't matter to Hogan . . . or Hollywood.
The fans still loved the "Hulkster," and the television and movie roles kept coming.

In 1990, Hogan appeared as himself on a
televised tribute to 50 years of Looney Tunes
cartoons, and in the movie *Gremlins 2: The New
Batch.*

In 1991, Hogan went back to Hollywood as
executive producer of *Suburban Commando*, in
which he played Shep Ramsey, an interstellar
superhero stranded on Earth. Unlike *No Holds
Barred*, Hogan starred alongside some better-
known Hollywood names: Christopher Lloyd
and Shelly Duvall. Like *No Holds Barred*, it got
terrible reviews. Noted film critic Roger Ebert
wrote: "Somebody was asking the other day, do
I ever get tired of going to the movies? Naw, I
said, I love movies and so some days it's not
really a job, it's more of a lucky break. But I
wasn't feeling lucky the day I saw *Suburban
Commando*, and you know what? By golly, by
the time it was over, I was feeling kind of tired
of going to the movies."

As Hogan spent more and more time making
movies, rumors circulated that he was feeling
kind of tired of going to the wrestling ring. Would
Hogan forsake his millions of Hulkamaniacs

to embark on a full-time movie career? Would he turn his back on the sport that had made him an international celebrity?

Hogan paid as little attention to the rumors as he did to the bad reviews, and so did Hollywood. Hogan—and Hollywood itself—were determined to find a place on the big screen for the Hulkster. After all, hadn't just about every notable actor starred in some terrible movies when he or she was starting out?

"As an entertainer, I've found my groove in the wrestling world," Hogan told *Newsday* in 1991. "I'm trying to use the same formula in the world of film because I didn't want to copy Arnold Schwarzenegger. I didn't want to fall into that groove of action-adventure, bloodthirsty, shoot-'em-up, kill-'em, a thousand dead people at your feet and you're the hero. I don't like dwelling on the negatives. I figure, why can't we dwell on our positives?"

In 1993, Hogan returned to the big screen in *Mr. Nanny*. He played Sean Armstrong, a former wrestler working as a bodyguard who gets mixed up in an espionage caper surrounding a secret microchip. The hook of the movie was painfully similar to *Kindergarten Cop*, which three years earlier starred Arnold Schwarzenegger. One reviewer called *Mr. Nanny* "one of the most monstrously agonizing motion pictures to come along this year."

The reviews may have bothered Hogan, but he no doubt received plenty of solace in what *People* magazine wrote in its October 14, 1991, issue: "As an action hero, the 38-year-old Hulkster is not about to terminate Arnold Schwarzenegger, but Hogan and his full-nelson comrades are laughing all the way to their brokers' offices. Thanks to TV and an annual gate of more than 8 million arena fans, the WWF empire is now worth an estimated $500 million."

Nobody was really sure what Hogan was worth, but this much was certain: he had come a long, long way from wrestling seven nights a week for $125.

That kind of success makes one a target. Not only of challengers in the wrestling ring, but of challengers in the courtroom.

5

LEGAL TURMOIL

Throughout the last years of the 1980s and into the earliest years of the 1990s, Hulk Hogan continued to be the man around whom the WWF revolved.

From January 23, 1984, through June 13, 1993, Hogan captured five WWF World heavyweight titles. In doing so, he defeated some of the sport's most formidable opponents: the Iron Sheik, Randy Savage, Sergeant Slaughter, The Undertaker, and Yokozuna.

From March 31, 1985, through April 4, 1993, Hogan was at the core of every WrestleMania extravaganza. Whether he lost a title, won a title, defended a title, settled a grudge, or initiated a feud, Hogan remained the focal point of the WWF's annual showcase—and, by and large, of the half-dozen or so pay-per-view events that occurred each year in addition to WrestleMania.

He also was the focal point of some disturbing legal situations.

On March 28, 1985, Hogan was in the midst of a whirlwind publicity tour for the first WrestleMania card, which was to take place three days later. For most of his public appearances during this important pre-WrestleMania sprint to the opening bell, Hogan was accompanied by Mr. T, who was to be

Hulk Hogan leaves a U.S. District Court in Uniondale, New York, on July 14, 1994, after testifying for the prosecution at the trial of WWF owner Vince McMahon Jr.

his tag team partner for the WrestleMania main event.

On this particular Thursday, Hogan and Mr. T were appearing on the Lifetime cable network television program *Hot Properties*. The interview show was hosted by comedian Richard Belzer, who would later receive acclaim for his acting on the popular dramatic television series *Homicide: Life in the Streets*.

Belzer's stand-up comedy was notable for its cynical view of the world, and the notion of him interviewing professional wrestlers was interesting. He was not the type of host who would simply allow Hogan and Mr. T to promote WrestleMania without verbally challenging them in some way.

Although some viewers stated that Belzer did little to mask his disdain for the mat sport, the interview went fine.

Until Belzer asked Hogan to demonstrate a hold.

Rising from the interview chairs, Hogan and Belzer took center stage. Hogan told the host that he was going to place Belzer in a front face-lock, a fairly rudimentary wrestling hold in which Hogan was to wrap his arm around Belzer's head and immobilize him.

Hogan carefully placed Belzer in the hold.

Belzer joked a bit.

Hogan evidently cinched down on the hold.

Belzer was immobilized . . . and then some.

The host visibly slumped in Hogan's arms, and the WWF World champion let Belzer slip to the hard floor. Belzer, unconscious, cracked his head on the floor. A pool of blood began to ooze visibly from beneath Belzer's head. Hogan quickly tried to revive him. Belzer was revived but was clearly not himself. He leaped to his feet, called for a commercial, and ran backstage, where he collapsed and was subsequently taken to a New York City hospital for treatment.

If Belzer watched WrestleMania, he did so with nine stitches in the back of his head. A lawsuit followed, in which the television host sought $5 million in damages. The suit was settled out of court, and neither party has since divulged the details of the settlement. It is widely speculated, however, that Belzer received a significant sum of money.

The lawsuit was the second major black eye for the WWF in just six weeks. On February 21, ABC's *20/20* program broadcast a story on professional wrestling. Although Hogan was not involved in the story, a former opponent of his was: "Dr. D" David Shultz was being interviewed by ABC reporter John Stossel. When Stossel said he thought wrestling was fake, Shultz hit the reporter twice in the head with open-handed slaps. Stossel later sued and received a $280,000 settlement from the WWF.

The WWF survived its 1985 problems and went on to experience incredible growth in popularity. But what goes up must come down, and as the 1990s began, it seemed that the bubble that was the WWF was about to burst.

And because Hulk Hogan was, in so many respects, synonymous with WWF success, his bubble seemed about to burst as well.

WrestleMania VII on March 24, 1991, was an amazing event. The United States, in the midst of the Persian Gulf War, was experiencing a rising tide of patriotism. So when then-WWF World champion Sergeant Slaughter began expressing his sympathies for Iraq, it became clear that he needed to be silenced. It became clear that Hogan was the man for the job. Not only did Hogan crush Slaughter, he captured his third WWF World title in the process.

But the WWF began experiencing criticism as it never had before. Many felt that it had made money at WrestleMania by capitalizing on the blood shed by American soldiers in the Persian Gulf. The all-American shine on Hogan was starting to tarnish just a bit.

Three months later, Dr. George T. Zahorian, a physician who had once served as the ringside physician for WWF events in Pennsylvania, was convicted on 12 counts of selling anabolic steroids to four pro wrestlers and a weight lifter. He subsequently received three years in prison, and the case started shock waves rippling through the WWF that would reverberate for years.

On July 16, less than three weeks after Zahorian was convicted, WWF head Vince McMahon held a press conference. He announced that all WWF stars would undergo mandatory testing for anabolic steroids as part of the federation's overall drug policy. That evening, Hogan appeared on *The Arsenio Hall Show* and declared: "I've trained 20 years, two hours a day, to look like I do. But the thing I am not, is I'm not a steroid abuser, and I do not use steroids."

The questions of steroid abuse would not go away, and neither would the WWF's legal problems. Allegations of sexual misconduct were leveled by former WWF employees. On March 13, 1992, McMahon appeared on CNN's *Larry King Live* to address those allegations, as well as the lingering questions of steroid abuse in the WWF. On July 31, WWF World champion Randy Savage appeared on *The Arsenio Hall Show* and said that yes, he did experiment with steroids, though he pointed out that the muscle-enhancing drugs were legal at the time he did.

On November 18, 1993, the runaway train crashed: McMahon was indicted on charges of possession of anabolic steroids and conspiracy to distribute anabolic steroids. If convicted on both counts, he would face up to eight years in prison and a half-million-dollar fine.

As McMahon awaited the trial, there were still more high-profile legal problems: Chuck Austin, a preliminary wrestler left paralyzed after a 1990 WWF tag team match in Florida, had sued the WWF. On April 29, 1994, he won a $26.7-million judgement against the federation.

There were problems inside the ring, too. Although Hogan had defeated Yokozuna on April 4, 1993, in Las Vegas to capture his fifth WWF World title, it was evident that the Hulkster was not taking the championship as seriously as he had the first time around. The evidence? A month after defeating Yokozuna, Hogan wrestled in Japan. He battled IWGP heavyweight champion the Great Muta, pinning his foe in the nontitle match. After the bout, Hogan made a comparison between the IWGP and WWF heavyweight titles. He likened the IWGP championship to a Rolls-Royce; by comparison, he said, the WWF belt was a Honda.

Perhaps the pressures of the WWF's legal problems were weighing on Hogan's massive shoulders, or perhaps he was growing weary of competing in the WWF in general. In either case, it seemed as if Hogan's days with the WWF were numbered.

Vince McMahon Jr. strolls with his wife Linda outside the federal court in Uniondale, New York, on July 22, 1994, as they await a verdict in McMahon's trial.

They were.

On July 5, 1994, McMahon's trial on steroid distribution charges began in Uniondale, New York. Hogan was called as a witness. During his testimony, Hogan contradicted the statements he had made three years earlier on *The Arsenio Hall Show*. He admitted to using steroids and testified that he shared them with McMahon while filming *No Holds Barred*.

The wrestling world was reeling, but it was hardly shocked. Hogan, after all, was only confirming in a court of law what many had suspected all along: that he, along with so many other muscular pro wrestlers, had used steroids to enhance their physiques.

McMahon was acquitted of the charges against him on July 22, following 16 hours of jury deliberation. The verdict saw spectators in the federal courtroom applaud, but the damage to the sport had been done. The damage to Hogan's reputation was irreversible. And the image of Hogan testifying in a trial against McMahon, the man who had made him wealthy and famous beyond imagination, was impossible to ignore.

Was Hogan worried about repercussions from the trial?

Hardly.

On June 11, less than four weeks before McMahon's trial began, Hogan had signed a contract to join WCW.

Wrestling history was about to be made again.

6 THE RENEGADE

As stunned as the wrestling world was by Hulk Hogan testifying against Vince McMahon, it was even more shocked by Hogan's defection from the WWF to WCW. After all, the WWF had given Hogan everything: riches, fame, respect, and a comfortable life for himself, his wife, and his children. Hogan leaving the WWF was unthinkable!

In 1994, however, the unthinkable was becoming commonplace in pro wrestling. The sport was undergoing fundamental changes. The lines between good guys and bad guys were blurring to the point of nonexistence. The wrestling world no longer consisted of rulebreakers and heroes—in fact, the rulebreaker had become the hero. The rise of wrestlers like Steve Austin and The Undertaker was beginning to pave the way for a new type of wrestling star, the antihero.

Hogan, however, remained his massively popular, thoroughly sportsmanlike self . . . for the moment.

His first WCW appearance, at Clash of the Champions XXVII on June 24, 1994, saw the Hulkster save WCW International champion Sting from a two-on-one attack by WCW World champion Ric "the Nature Boy" Flair and "Sensational" Sherri Martel. Later in the evening, Flair defeated Sting to unify the two titles.

Just three days after testifying against WWF owner Vince McMahon Jr., Hogan defeated Ric Flair to capture his first WCW World heavyweight title at the July 17, 1994, Bash at the Beach.

Hogan, as usual, remained the centerpiece of the event. "I'm in WCW because I've got some unfinished business with Flair," Hogan said, and indeed he had.

On October 22, 1991, Flair and Hogan had battled each other for the first time ever. Flair had entered the WWF about six weeks earlier, on September 10, with the stated intent of capturing the WWF World title, which Hogan had held at the time. The wrestling world had salivated at the prospect of longtime NWA mainstay Flair battling WWF kingpin Hogan. The Hulkster had lost that first encounter by countout and never forgotten it. Flair had gone on to capture two WWF World titles.

So when it came time for WCW's Bash at the Beach pay-per-view event, on July 17, 1994, Hogan was ready. It took him 21 minutes and 50 seconds to defeat the Nature Boy and capture his first WCW World title . . . just three days after he had testified against McMahon.

The Flair-Hogan war consumed most of the Hulkster's first year in WCW. Immediately after the Bash at the Beach match, a Hogan-Flair rematch was signed for the nationally televised Clash of the Champions XXVIII card on August 24. Early in the card, Hogan was viciously attacked by a masked man. It looked as if the Hulkster would not be able to wrestle that night, but he courageously staggered out of his hospital bed and made his way to the ring, where he lost to Flair by countout.

A loser-must-retire cage match between Hogan and Flair was signed for the October 24 Halloween Havoc pay-per-view card. Hogan pinned the Nature Boy to retain his title and end Flair's career, but jubilance turned to

shock when it was revealed that the masked man who had ambushed him at the Clash was in fact his close friend, Brutus Beefcake.

Hogan subsequently pinned Beefcake at the Starrcade '94 pay-per-view on December 27, and Beefcake subsequently begged for forgiveness. Hogan refused to cave in to his old friend. Besides, he was too busy battling Big Van Vader, and later Flair, who was reinstated by WCW in the spring of 1995.

Hogan defeated Vader in a steel cage match at Bash at the Beach on July 16, 1995, but the match marked the end of Hogan's relentless string of successes since arriving in WCW.

The Hulkster's fortunes were about to turn.

A new rookie arrived in WCW in 1995. Aptly named The Giant, he stood 7' 4" and weighed 430 pounds. Ironically, he was from Tampa, Florida, the city Hogan called home.

Hulk Hogan and Randy Savage stand with their friend Kevin Greene, center, of the Pittsburgh Steelers, who came to cheer them on at the Clash of the Champions on January 23, 1996 in Las Vegas. Hogan and Savage lost their match against Ric Flair and The Giant and did not get a chance at the WCW World tag team title.

It didn't take long for The Giant and Hogan to cross paths, and their battles were reminiscent of Hogan's battles with Andre the Giant more than a decade earlier. This Giant, however, was leaner and meaner than Andre and possessed a remarkable level of athletic skill for such a large man.

At the Halloween Havoc pay-per-view card on October 29, 1995, WCW World champion Hogan lost to The Giant by disqualification. According to a clause in the match contract, the title was allowed to change hands on a disqualification. However, the clause was ruled invalid because the disqualification had come about as the result of the interference of Jimmy Hart.

The result of all the confusion? The title was declared vacant and put up for grabs in a three-ring, 60-man battle royal, to be held at the World War III pay-per-view on November 26. The Giant was thrilled. Not only had he defeated Hogan, he had made sure that Hogan was no longer World champion.

The Giant also made sure that Hogan would not regain the title. At World War III, after The Giant was eliminated from the battle royal, he pulled Hogan out of the ring, thus destroying the Hulkster's hopes of regaining the title that night. Randy Savage went on to win the belt.

Hogan's fortunes in the ring continued to slide. He teamed with Savage to battle Flair and The Giant at the nationally televised Clash of the Champions XXXII card on January 23, 1996, but was pinned by Flair. Hogan found himself in a bitter feud with Kevin Sullivan which, even if he won decisively, would take him nowhere.

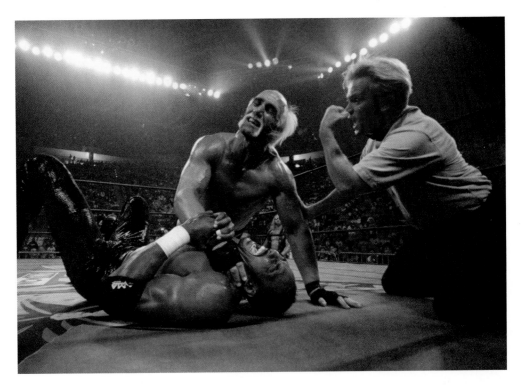

It was time for Hogan to step back and take a break. He left WCW in the spring of 1996 to film a movie, and while he was gone, the face of wrestling changed again.

Scott Hall and Kevin Nash, superstars in the WWF known respectively as Razor Ramon and Diesel, had left McMahon's federation and invaded WCW as the Outsiders. Hall and Nash were obnoxious, arrogant, and stunningly successful.

For the Bash at the Beach pay-per-view event held on July 7, 1996, Hall and Nash signed to compete in a six-man match against Savage, Sting, and Lex Luger. They told WCW audiences that they had a third man for their team and that their mystery partner would be a famous former WWF star.

Hollywood Hogan puts a chokehold on the neck of Utah Jazz basketball star Karl Malone at a pay-per-view match held in San Diego on July 12, 1998. Hogan continued to attract celebrities to professional wrestling in the 1990s, even recruiting Dennis Rodman of the Chicago Bulls into the NWO.

Hulk Hogan lifts his costar Loni Anderson during a premiere party in Los Angeles for their 1998 film Three Ninjas: High Noon at Mega Mountain. *Hogan stayed true to his Hollywood form during the late 1990s and continued to star in movies and TV shows, while at the same time maintaining his popularity as an NWO renegade.*

The wrestling world was rampant with rumors, most of them ultimately asking the same question: would Hulk Hogan be the third Outsider?

When match time rolled around, no third partner was to be seen. Hall and Nash gamely took on the trio of Savage, Sting, and Luger in a handicap bout. After Luger was injured in the bout and carried away on a stretcher, Hall and Nash delivered a brutal beating to Sting and Savage.

Suddenly, Hogan came running from the dressing room. The fans cheered, expecting the Hulkster to save Sting and Savage.

Instead, he legdropped Savage and revealed himself to be the mysterious third partner of the Outsiders. After more than 10 years as the most beloved individual the sport had ever known, Hulk Hogan was once again a rule-breaker!

With Hall and Nash standing alongside him, the Hulkster gave a postmatch interview that was a stunner.

"This right here is the future of wrestling. You can call this the New World Order [NWO] of wrestling, brother. These are the men I want as my friends. They're the new blood of professional wrestling, brother, and not only are we going to take over the whole wrestling business, with Hulk Hogan and the new blood, the monster with me, we will destroy everything in our path.

"For two years, brother, for two years I held my head high. I did everything for the kids. The reception I got when I came out here? You fans can stick it, brother, because if it wasn't for Hulk Hogan, you people wouldn't be here. If it wasn't for Hulk Hogan, [WCW executive vice president] Eric Bischoff would still be selling meat from a truck in Minneapolis, and if it wasn't for Hulk Hogan, all these Johnny-come-latelys that you see out here wrestling wouldn't be here."

Hulk Hogan had told the fans to "stick it!" As amazingly as Hulkamania had begun on January 23, 1984, it had just as amazingly come crashing down on July 7, 1996.

Perhaps even more amazing, Hogan's career had been revitalized like never before!

The NWO lived up to Hogan's prediction and truly did destroy everything in its path. Hogan regained the WCW World title from The Giant on August 10 and desecrated the belt itself by spray-painting "NWO" on the championship gold. The Giant, evidently realizing that discretion is the better part of valor, subsequently joined the NWO (he would later defect back to WCW). Other top-name wrestlers followed suit: Ted DiBiase, Syxx, Michael Wall Street, Big Bubba, Marcus Bagwell, Masa Chono, and WCW executive vice president Bischoff himself.

The NWO was the hub around which everything in WCW revolved. Wrestlers in WCW were asked to choose sides. "Are you WCW or NWO?" became the litmus test question. Wrestlers entering WCW were watched closely to see if

On November 26, 1998, at age 45, Hulk Hogan announced his retirement on The Tonight Show with Jay Leno. *Yet by 1999, Hogan had returned to the wrestling ring—he captured the WCW World title from Kevin Nash on January 4, lost it to Ric Flair on March 14, and was determined to win it back again.*

they had NWO tendencies. On November 25, 1996, Bischoff turned up the pressure, announcing that all WCW wrestlers had 30 days to convert their WCW contracts to NWO contracts or risk becoming NWO targets.

At Starrcade '96, Roddy Piper battled—and defeated—Hogan in a nontitle steel cage match. The match marked Hogan's first clear defeat in nearly six years, but it had no measurable effect on the momentum the NWO was building.

The NWO vs. WCW war consumed the sport, and newly renamed "Hollywood" Hogan loved every minute of it. His WCW World title reign ended briefly, when he was defeated by Lex Luger on August 4, 1997, in Detroit, but Hollywood regained the belt just five days later.

And as he did in the '80s, Hogan grabbed mainstream headlines in the '90s. Most notably, he did so by recruiting Chicago Bulls basketball star Dennis Rodman into the NWO. Rodman teamed with Hogan at the July 13, 1997, Bash at the Beach pay-per-view card to battle Lex Luger and The Giant. Hogan lost the match for his team, though, when he submitted to Luger's "torture rack" backbreaker. His in-ring troubles were just beginning.

While the NWO continued to dominate, there were troubles there, too. The group had split into two opposing factions: NWO Hollywood and the NWO Wolfpac. The overall allegiance of wrestlers to Hogan's leadership was eroding.

Meanwhile, inside the ring, Hogan continued to slump. At Halloween Havoc on October 26, 1997, Hogan again lost to Piper, again in a cage match. At Starrcade '97 on December 28, Hogan lost the WCW World title to Sting.

Hollywood rebounded in 1998, capturing the WCW World title from Randy Savage on April 20, 1998, just one day after Savage had won the title from Sting at the Spring Stampede pay-per-view event. Hogan's fourth WCW reign would be the shortest of them all, as it would come to an end less than three months later at the hands of rookie sensation Bill Goldberg on July 6, 1998.

The loss to Goldberg was devastating. Hogan turned to Dennis Rodman as his partner for the July 12 Bash at the Beach pay-per-view match against Dallas Page and basketball star Karl Malone. The team won when Hogan pinned Page, but clearly something was missing. The fire that had burned so brightly when Hogan joined the NWO was starting to dim.

On November 26, on *The Tonight Show with Jay Leno*, Hogan announced his retirement. In the wake of former wrestler Jesse Ventura's victory in the race for the governorship of Minnesota, Hogan said he was running for president in the year 2000. Everyone laughed, but dismissed the presidential bid as just another publicity ploy.

"I think everybody should be smart enough to know your limitations," Hogan said in a 1993 interview. "They've got certain people they call living legends. Sometimes we call them living leeches, they just hang around forever and milk the business and sometimes embarrass themselves, they get so old and still wrestle. If it ever gets to that point, I wish somebody will tell me. I still think I've got a few good years left."

As 1999 got underway, the 46-year-old Hogan ignored his national retirement announcement and was waging war with the 50-year-old Flair over the WCW World title that Hogan had regained by defeating Kevin Nash on January 4.

"I sat back for a couple of months and watched the ratings plummet," Hogan told a Chicago morning radio audience, "and these so-called superstars of five-to-nine years try to carry the load. So I'm back and ready to put money back in everyone's pockets."

Undoubtedly, Hogan would love to begin the 21st century on top of the pro wrestling world. He changed the sport in the 1980s, changed it again in the 1990s, and it wouldn't come as a surprise to anyone if he changed it yet again in 2000 and beyond.

But no matter what happens in the years to come, it's impossible to deny that Hulk Hogan has left the kind of indelible mark on pro wrestling that few athletes are privileged to make in their chosen sport. Hogan has done for pro wrestling what Muhammad Ali did for boxing, what Jack Nicklaus did for golf, and what Michael Jordan did for basketball.

We aren't likely to see his kind ever again.

Chronology

1953   Born Terry Bollea in Augusta, Georgia, on August 11.

1978   Makes his pro debut under the name "Terry Boulder."

1979   Signs with the WWF; Wrestles under the name "Incredible Hulk Hogan."

1980   Battles Andre the Giant in New York's Shea Stadium.

1981   Signs with the AWA.

1983   Returns to the WWF.

1984   Defeats the Iron Sheik in Madison Square Garden to capture his first WWF World title and "Hulkamania" is born.

1988   Loses the WWF World title to Andre the Giant.

1989   Appears in his first movie, *No Holds Barred*; Captures his second WWF World title from Randy Savage.

1990   Loses the WWF World title to the Ultimate Warrior.

1991   Captures his third WWF World title from Sergeant Slaughter; Loses the WWF World title to The Undertaker; Captures his fourth WWF World title from The Undertaker—the following day, the WWF declares the title vacant.

1993   Captures his fifth WWF World title from Yokozuna; Loses the WWF World title to Yokozuna.

1994   Signs with WCW; Testifies against Vince McMahon during McMahon's trial on charges of steroid distribution; Captures his first WCW World title from Ric Flair; WCW World title declared vacant.

1996   Turns rulebreaker and forms the NWO with Scott Hall and Kevin Nash; As "Hollywood" Hogan, captures his second WCW World title from The Giant.

1997   Loses the WCW World title to Lex Luger; Captures his third WCW World title from Lex Luger; Loses the WCW World title to Sting.

1998   Captures his fourth WCW World title from Randy Savage; Loses the WCW World title to Bill Goldberg.

1999   Captures his fifth WCW World title from Kevin Nash; Loses the WCW World title to Ric Flair.

Further Reading

Humber, Larry. *WWF Presents All About Hulk Hogan Fact Book.* New York: Checkerboard Press, 1991.

Janoff, Barry. *Hulk Hogan: Eye of the Tiger.* New York: Children's Press, 1986.

Neil, Abbot. *Hulkamania! Hulk Hogan: America's Hero.* New York: Pocket Books, 1985.

Rosenbaum, Dave. "The Starrcade Scandal! We Hate to Say It, but …Give the Belt Back to Hogan!" *Inside Wrestling Digest* (Spring 1998): 36–40.

Sanford, William R. *Hulk Hogan.* New York: Crestwood House, 1986.

Straightshooter, The. "Resurrecting the Hulk." *WOW Magazine* (May 1999): 130–135.

World Wrestling Federation. *Hulkamania: The Official Biography of Hulk Hogan.* New York: Bantam/Doubleday/Dell, 1985.

Index

Photo Credits

MATT HUNTER has spent 18 years writing about professional wrestling. In addition to this biography of Hulk Hogan, the author has written *Superstars of Pro Wrestling* and a biography of Jesse Ventura. He has also interviewed countless wrestlers on national television, photographed innumerable bouts from ringside, and written more magazine articles about the mat sport than he cares to calculate.